Killer Whales
and Other Toothed Whales

Concept and Product Development: Editorial Options, Inc.
Series Designer: Karen Donica
Book Author: Julie A. Fenton

For information on other World Book
products, visit us at our Web site at
http://www.worldbook.com

For information on sales to schools and libraries
in the United States, call 1-800-975-3250.

For information on sales to schools and libraries
in Canada, call 1-800-837-5365.

World Book, Inc.
233 N. Michigan Avenue
Chicago, IL 60601

Library of Congress Cataloging-in-Publication Data

Killer whales and other toothed whales.
        p. cm. -- (World Book's animals of the world)
    ISBN 0-7166-1215-1 -- ISBN 0-7166-1211-9 (set)
    1. Killer whale--Juvenile literature. 2. Toothed whales--Juvenile literature. [1. Killer
whale. 2. Toothed whales. 3. Whales.] I. World Book, Inc. II. Series.

    QL737.C432 K56 2001
    599.53'6--dc21   2001017530

Printed in Singapore

1 2 3 4 5 6 7 8 9 05 04 03 02 01

Killer Whales
and Other Toothed Whales

Why do they call me "Killer"?

World Book, Inc.
A Scott Fetzer Company
Chicago

Contents

Why do people sometimes call us show-offs?

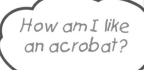

How am I like an acrobat?

What Is a Toothed Whale?

As you might expect, a toothed whale has teeth. Oddly enough, some toothed whales have only one tooth, while others have more than 200. All whales belong to an order of mammals called cetaceans *(suh TAY shuhnz).* Cetaceans are divided into two suborders: toothed whales and baleen *(BAY leen)* whales. Baleen whales have no teeth at all.

The toothed whale you see here is a killer whale. It belongs to the family of whales called ocean dolphins. Bottle-nosed dolphins and pilot whales also belong to this family. There are several other families of toothed whales. These include porpoises, river dolphins, beaked whales, sperm whales, and belugas *(buh LOO guhz)* and narwhals.

Killer whale

Where in the World Do Toothed Whales Live?

Like fish, whales spend their entire lives in water. Their bodies are sleek and shaped like torpedoes. They're perfectly suited for life in a watery world, where swimming is the best way to get around.

Toothed whales live in all the oceans of the world. Some, however, prefer deep water to shallow water. Sperm whales like deep water—as do beaked whales.

Dall's porpoises also like the open seas. But most other porpoises seem to prefer shallow coastal waters. They are often seen in harbors and other inlets. Belugas and narwhals also hug the coast. But they like the pack ice around the North Pole.

River dolphins live in some of the world's large river systems. Ocean dolphins prefer the open seas. But, only the killer whale has a truly worldwide habitat. It is found in all the oceans and seas of the world.

Deep, open sea

Shallow, coastal waters

Icy Arctic waters

Rivers

How Do Whales Differ from Other Mammals?

This diagram shows some parts of a killer whale's body. All whales are mammals, but they differ from other mammals in some obvious ways.

Most mammals have four legs. A whale has no hind legs. And instead of front legs, a whale has flippers. These help the whale steer and keep its balance. A whale also has a tail fin that spreads out into two wings, or flukes. On its back, this killer whale has a triangular-shaped fin, called a dorsal fin. Fish have fins—but most mammals do not.

Most mammals have hair on their bodies. But toothed whales have only a few bristles—or none at all. Many toothed whales have long snouts, called beaks, and bulging foreheads, or melons.

Whales are like other mammals in some ways, however. They have lungs and breathe air—just as you do. They are warm-blooded, or make their own body heat. Babies nurse on their mothers' milk.

Diagram of Killer Whale

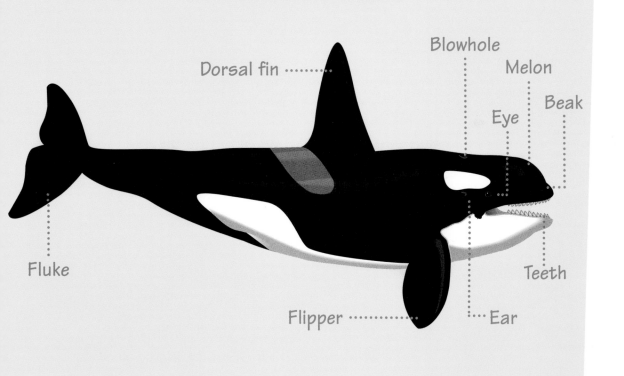

Dorsal fin ·········

Blowhole

Melon

Beak

Eye

Fluke

Flipper ··············

Ear

Teeth

What Is So Striking About a Killer Whale?

Of all toothed whales, a killer whale is perhaps the most striking. One reason is its size. A male can grow to be 30 feet (9 meters) long. And it can weigh up to 10 tons (9 metric tons). That's really big!

As you can see, a killer whale also has distinct markings. The whale's back and tail are a glossy black. But its belly is a bright white. There is also a white oval patch above and behind each eye. This patch is called the eyespot. The killer whale also has a gray saddle patch in the center of its back.

A killer whale's coloring helps to camouflage *(KAM uh flahzh),* or hide, the animal as it hunts for food in the ocean. When you look down at a killer whale, its black back blends into the dark water. When you look up at the whale from underwater, its white belly is hard to see against the light sky. From the side, the black-and-white markings look like sunlight hitting the water. Its camouflage coloring makes the killer whale a sneaky hunter!

Killer whale

Is That Killer Whale a He or a She?

At first glance, you might think male and female killer whales look alike. But they do not! If you look carefully, you'll see a difference in their fins.

Look at the two killer whales in the picture. One is a male, or bull. The other is a female, or cow. Each has a dorsal fin. But the two fins are quite different. The cow's dorsal fin is curved. The bull's fin is not curved. And the bull's fin can grow to be 6 feet (1.8 meters) high. The cow's dorsal fin is much shorter. It grows to only about 3 feet (0.9 meter).

Another way to tell a bull from a cow is to look at the size of the animal's body. Bulls are much longer and bulkier than cows. Bulls also have bigger flippers.

Killer whales

How Does a Killer Whale Stay Warm?

Most mammals that live in cold climates have thick fur to keep them warm. A killer whale has no fur. But it does have thick skin. This skin is lined with blubber. Blubber is a layer of fatty tissue just beneath a marine mammal's skin. The blubber of a killer whale is 3 to 4 inches (7.6 to 10.1 centimeters) thick.

Blubber acts like an extra layer of clothing. It covers most of the killer whale's body. Only the flippers, the flukes, and the dorsal fin lack blubber. Blubber keeps out the cold and traps heat in. Without blubber, the whale couldn't survive in icy waters.

A killer whale can also turn its blubber into energy, which heats up the animal's body. The whale can live off this fatty layer when it can't find food. When there is plenty of food, the whale will build its layer of blubber back up.

Killer whale

How Does a Killer Whale Breathe?

A killer whale breathes through a nostril called a blowhole. The blowhole is at the top of the animal's head. This is a great place for a nose. It allows the killer whale to swim without having to lift its whole head out of the water to breathe.

As a killer whale swims, it brings the front of its body out of the water. It snorts the used-up air out through the blowhole. This is called a "blow." Before diving, the whale takes in a fresh supply of air. Then, as it dives, a special muscle closes the nostril inside the blowhole so that water does not get in.

It can be exciting to see a blow. It looks like a spout of white, misty spray. All cetaceans blow. The bigger the animal, the bigger the blow!

Killer whales

Are Killer Whales Social Animals?

Killer whales are very social animals. They often live together. And they survive by working together. A group of killer whale families is called a pod. Killer whales travel with others in their pod. Members of a pod hunt, play, and rest together.

The founder of each family is often one of the older females. Other family members include the female's offspring and close relatives. Pod members communicate by making sounds—as well as with body language.

A killer whale usually lives in the same pod for its entire life. Can you imagine living your whole life in the same house with your mother, brothers, sisters, aunts, uncles, and cousins? That's how it is for killer whales. These mammals show great affection for one another. They develop strong ties with other family members.

Pod of killer whales

What Sounds Do Killer Whales Make?

Killer whales make many different sounds. They make rapid clicking sounds. They also whistle, screech, squeak, and make other noises. Some of their calls can be heard from several miles away.

Scientists think that killer whales use their whistles and most other calls to signal each other. The whales signal to warn others, to attract mates, to start a hunt, and to communicate for other reasons. Killer whales use their clicks for a special purpose—to locate prey.

Each pod of killer whales has its own set of sounds, or dialect. Related pods have dialects that are also related. Killer whales living in related pods can "understand" each other's dialects. Those living in unrelated pods have very different dialects.

Killer whales

How Does Clicking Help Killer Whales Hunt?

To find food, a killer whale may use echolocation *(EKH oh loh KAY shuhn).* To do this, the whale first makes several clicks. The clicks leave the animal's body through the melon, which directs the sounds forward. The clicks spread through the water until they hit an object, such as a fish. Then they bounce off the object and return as echoes. In a flash, the whale can tell where a fish is. The whale also knows the fish's size, shape, speed, and direction.

Killer whales use echolocation to find fish and other smaller prey. But they don't always use echolocation to hunt. To find larger prey, such as seals, killer whales simply use their eyes.

Most toothed whales use echolocation at some time. Scientists think that echolocation is a learned skill. It does not come naturally. Echolocating is a very important skill—especially for whales that hunt in deep, dark waters or in murky rivers.

Echolocation

How Else Do Killer Whales Find Food?

Killer whales often hunt together in packs. They may work as a team to herd a school of fish against the shore. Killer whales attack not only fish but also porpoises, seals, sea turtles, penguins, and even large baleen whales. Once the killer whales have trapped their prey, they share their catch with one another.

Sometimes a killer whale surprises its victim by tipping an ice floe, a floating sheet of ice. The seal or penguin on the floe slips from the ice. The killer whale uses its cone-shaped teeth to grab the prey. A killer whale may have as many as 52 teeth. But it doesn't use its teeth to chew. Instead, the whale drags its meal into the water and swallows it whole.

Killer whales are fierce hunters. They can chase down most sea creatures. It is nearly impossible to escape the jaws of a hungry killer whale! That's how the animal got the name killer whale.

Killer whales

27

Do Killer Whales Stay Put or Wander?

Some killer whales stay in one place. Others travel great distances. It all depends on the type of pod the whales live in.

One kind of pod is a transient pod. Killer whales in these pods travel long distances. The pods are usually small. They may have only seven members. Killer whales in these pods feed mostly on larger sea animals, such as seals and porpoises. Some transient pods even attack large whales.

Resident pods do not move around so much. They are easier to observe. In fact, much of what we know about killer whales comes from studying these pods. Resident pods range in size from 5 to 25 members. Whales in these pods eat mainly fish.

When a pod gets too large, a female and her offspring may leave to start a new pod. Sometimes, the related pods come together to travel and feed. It's like a family reunion for killer whales!

Killer whales
on the move

Why Do Killer Whales Spyhop?

Here you see a killer whale spyhopping. In a spyhop, the whale points its head straight up out of the water. Then it sinks—but without much of a splash.

Scientists think that killer whales learn to spyhop at an early age. The whales probably do this to see what's going on around them. Killer whales do have fairly good eyesight, especially out of water. And spyhopping is a good way to seek out large prey, such as seals and penguins.

Many other kinds of whales also spyhop. It's quite a sight to see!

Killer whale
spyhopping

What Is Lobtailing?

The killer whale you see here is lobtailing. In a lobtail, the whale points its head straight down into the water. It raises its flukes into the air and waves them back and forth a few times. Then, with a loud *woosh*, the animal slaps its flukes on the surface of the water.

No one knows for sure why whales lobtail. Lobtailing may be a way of communicating. Whales may lobtail to warn unfriendly whales to stay away. Or, whales may lobtail to alert members within a pod that danger is nearby.

Lobtailing is as amazing to watch as spyhopping. Many people go whale watching, hoping to see the whales make these moves.

Killer whale lobtailing

What Is Life Like for a Calf?

A baby killer whale is called a calf. Getting born is hard for the calf, and it's hard for the mother, too. Like most mammals, whales do not lay eggs. Females give birth to their young—underwater!

When it's time to give birth, the mother floats up toward the surface of the water. Usually, the baby is born tail first. The calf's head comes out last. But because it has no air in its lungs, the newborn calf must quickly get to the surface. It needs to breathe!

Right after her baby is born, the mother pushes it up to the surface of the water. There, the calf fills its lungs with air. Then it can return to its mother and begin to nurse. The calf drinks rich milk from its mother's teats. These teats are tucked away inside slits on her belly.

Killer whale
calf nursing

 35

Do Killer Whales Make Good Mothers?

Killer whales make excellent mothers. They care for their calves for at least a year—and sometimes longer. During that time, the calves depend on their mothers for both food and protection.

A killer whale calf always swims alongside its mother. It keeps up by riding on its mother's waves. The flow of water over the mother's body helps pull the calf along. The calf uses less energy. This allows both the mother and her baby to keep up with a traveling pod.

Sometimes a mother must go off to hunt for food. She leaves her baby with other adult females, called aunts. The aunts protect the calf from sharks and other whales. They also play with the calf. The aunts make great baby sitters!

Killer whale mother and calf

What Is So Unusual About Pilot Whales?

Pilot whales are big—but not nearly so big as killer whales. A pilot whale grows to about 21 feet (6 meters) in length; it may weigh 2 1/2 tons (2.3 metric tons). What makes a pilot whale unusual is its head. A pilot whale has a long, stocky body and a large, bulging forehead.

Pilot whales are very social animals. They often swim in a single-file line. It looks as if they are playing "Follow the Leader." Sometimes, this leads to disaster. If the leader swims into water that is too shallow, it may not be able to get back out into deeper water. The pilot whale becomes stranded! Others following it may become stranded, too.

Pilot whale

Do Bottle-Nosed Dolphins Go to School?

Bottle-nosed dolphins belong to the same family as killer whales and pilot whales. They, too, live and travel in social groups. Some people call this group a pod, but others call it a school. A school usually has about 12 dolphins. Some schools may combine to form a herd of up to 1,000 dolphins.

A bottle-nosed dolphin school is not just a place to live. It's also a place to learn. Young calves learn by imitating their mothers or other adult dolphins. Calves turn, dive, and surface—right along with the adults.

Play is also important to bottle-nosed dolphins. They enjoy leaping and tail splashing. Sometimes, they even walk backward on their tails! Young dolphins like to play by chasing each other around. But if play gets out of hand, a mother may warn a youngster by butting it with her head.

Bottle-nosed dolphins

How Do Bottle-Nosed Dolphins Hunt?

Bottle-nosed dolphins hunt in several different ways. How they hunt seems to depend on where they are at the time.

In the open ocean, bottle-nosed dolphins often form hunting herds. The dolphins circle a school of fish. Then they splash frantically to move the fish closer and closer together. Once the fish are tightly packed, the dolphins can take turns feeding.

Closer to shore, dolphins may drive a school of fish toward a rocky reef. Dolphins have even been known to beach themselves and grab their prey.

Bottle-nosed dolphins also hunt alone. A lone hunter may hit a fish with its flukes. Then it grabs the stunned fish and enjoys a quick meal.

Bottle-nosed dolphin

Which Dolphins Whirl and Twirl?

Spinner dolphins were named for the midair spins they do. Spinner dolphins can whirl and twirl—just like acrobats. How do they do this? First, the dolphin makes a dive. Then it leaps straight up into the air. It may leap 10 feet (3 meters) high. Then it spins— sometimes seven times in one leap.

Most other kinds of dolphins can somersault, or flip head over tail. But a spinner dolphin is the only one that can spin with its nose pointed to the sky and its tail to the water.

Spinner dolphins may perform such stunts to communicate with the schoolmates. They may be letting the others know where to find fish. Or, they may be jumping just for the fun of it.

Spinner dolphins are unusual in another way. They have more teeth than any other whale. A spinner dolphin may have up to 252 teeth!

Spinner dolphin

How Do Common Dolphins Sleep?

The common dolphins you see here are probably sleeping. How can you tell? A sleeping dolphin usually rests at or near the surface of the water. That way, the dolphin is not too far from the air it needs to breathe.

A sleeping dolphin usually has one eye closed. The dolphin's breathing rate slows down. Still, it seems to be aware of the fact that it is breathing. When you sleep, you are not aware of your breathing. You don't need to be conscious in order to breathe. But many scientists think that dolphins do need to be conscious.

Scientists also think that dolphins (and all other whales) sleep with one side of the brain resting at a time. The side that is awake controls the dolphin's breathing. It also controls the animal's movement. Resting one side of the brain at a time makes it possible to sleep underwater.

Common dolphins

Is It a Porpoise or a Dolphin?

You know that all toothed whales have teeth. But the teeth of a porpoise are different from those of a dolphin.

A dolphin has pointy, cone-shaped teeth. But a porpoise has rounded teeth. A porpoise has a smaller head than a dolphin does. And a porpoise has a rounded snout. Most porpoises also have small dorsal fins. The finless porpoise, as you might guess, has no dorsal fin at all.

Some porpoises are quite shy—but not the Dall's porpoises you see here. The Dall's porpoise is active all the time, and it seems to like to show off. Dall's porpoises often approach boats filled with whale watchers. The porpoises swim around the boats and may even ride the waves that the boats make.

Dall's porpoises

What Is a Beaked Whale?

Here you see a Baird's beaked whale. Most beaked whales have long, slender bodies. Many have only two teeth in their lower jaws. Most have no upper teeth at all.

A Baird's beaked whale can be up to 42 feet (13 meters) long. It's probably the largest of the beaked whales. It has a long beak—which looks a lot like the beak of a bottled-nosed dolphin. Males of this species have two pairs of teeth in their lower jaws. Scientists think that beaked whales use their teeth for fighting rather than for feeding. They may feed by sucking up their prey, which consists mostly of squid.

Most beaked whales live offshore, in deep waters. Of all whales, beaked whales are among the deepest divers. And their dives can last more than an hour. But they are not very fast swimmers.

Baird's beaked whale

51

Which River Dolphin Swims Upside Down?

This is an Amazon river dolphin. And yes, it is swimming upside down. Scientists aren't sure why Amazon river dolphins do this. The humps on their backs may help them feel around the river bottom to find food.

Swimming upside down may also help the dolphins see. Even though their eyes are small, these dolphins do have good eyesight. But their puffy cheeks may be a problem. It's hard to look down over those cheeks! The dolphins may be able to see prey better while swimming on their backs.

River dolphins usually live in fresh water or in water that is only slightly salty. Amazon river dolphins may be bright pink, bluish-gray, or off-white in color. They have humps instead of dorsal fins. And they have long, narrow beaks that they use for feeding.

Amazon river dolphin

53

Which Toothed Whale Has the Fewest Teeth?

The honor of being the whale with the fewest teeth goes to the narwhal. Look at the long, spiral tusk on this male narwhal. This tooth, or tusk, grows to about 8 feet (2.4 meters) long. It is made of ivory. But no one is sure what the tusk is for! It may be used in fighting. Or, it may be just for show.

All narwhals lack teeth inside their mouths. They probably capture prey by sucking. And, since they can't chew, they must then swallow the prey whole. Their prey includes fish, shrimps, and squid.

Although narwhals don't have teeth inside their mouths, they do have teeth. Both males and females have two teeth buried in their upper jaws. Only one tooth—the left tooth of the male—ever grows so that it can be seen. But what a tooth that is!

Narwhals

Which Toothed Whales Are All White?

Belugas are white when they are fully grown. The name *beluga* comes from a Russian word that means "white." Because of its color, the beluga is sometimes called the white whale.

Belugas are also known as sea canaries. That's because of the chirping sounds they make. Belugas live in the Arctic, where they search for prey such as fish, squid, crabs, and shrimp. Because they live in such a cold climate, belugas have extra thick layers of blubber to keep them warm.

Belugas are closely related to narwhals. But there is one very obvious difference. A beluga has many more teeth—from 32 to 40.

Adult beluga

Who Is the King of Toothed Whales?

A killer whale is big—but a sperm whale is even bigger. It can weigh as much as 55 tons (50 metric tons). An adult male sperm whale grows to about 60 feet (18 meters) long. That's twice the length of a killer whale! In size, the sperm whale is indeed the king of toothed whales.

Sperm whales also make the deepest and the longest dives of all toothed whales. Sperm whales dive to find their favorite prey—deep-water squids. Scientists think the whales may have some terrible battles with giant squids. Scientists think this because of the scars they have seen on the bodies of the whales.

Sperm whales spend most of their lives in a nursery school or a bachelor school. A nursery school is made up of adult females and their young. A bachelor school is made up of young males only. When a male sperm whale becomes an adult, he leaves the bachelor school and lives on his own.

58

Sperm whales

Are Toothed Whales in Danger?

The toothed whales most in danger are the river dolphins. People have killed many of these animals. People have also destroyed the animals' habitats. Scientists fear that the Baiji dolphins of China may soon become extinct.

The vaquita *(vuh KEE tuh)* porpoise, which lives in the Gulf of California, is also highly endangered. There may be only a few hundred of them left.

Sperm whales have been endangered for over 30 years. These great animals had been hunted almost to the point of extinction. Then, in 1984, a law was passed to ban commercial whaling. It is hoped that this law will help the sperm whales continue to increase in numbers.

Conservationists have been working hard to save the whales. But some whalers, as well as some nations, continue to hunt whales. And so the future of these magnificent animals remains uncertain.

Baiji dolphin

61

Toothed Whale Fun Facts

→ A killer whale is often called an orca. This comes from the whale's scientific name, *Orcinus orca.*

→ Scientists can tell a toothed whale's age by counting growth layers on its teeth. Each layer stands for one year!

→ The false killer whale is a kind of dolphin that looks like a real killer whale. But it is smaller and lacks the white spots.

→ A beluga whale changes color with age—from dark gray at birth to pure white as an adult.

→ You can tell a toothed whale from a baleen whale by counting blowholes. A toothed whale has one, but a baleen whale has two.

→ The narwhal is sometimes called the "unicorn of the sea."

→ A sperm whale has teeth only in its lower jaw. These fit into sockets in the whale's upper jaw.

→ The deepest known dive by a mammal was 6,560 feet (2,000 meters). It was made by a sperm whale.

Glossary

baleen whale A whale with comblike plates instead of teeth for feeding. The plates filter small prey from the water.

blowhole The opening in the head of a whale, a dolphin, or a porpoise that enables it to breathe.

blubber Thick fat under the skin of sea animals that keeps them warm and stores energy.

breaching Leaping out of the water and crashing back with a splash.

dorsal fin Raised part of the backs of many whales, dolphins, and porpoises.

echolocation The process of locating distant or unseen objects by means of sound waves.

extinct No longer existing.

eyespot A white oval patch behind each eye of a killer whale.

flukes The two flattened halves of the tail of a whale, a dolphin, or a porpoise.

lobtailing The forceful slapping of the flukes against the water while most of the animal remains below the surface.

mammal A warm-blooded animal that feeds its young on the mother's milk.

melon The bulging forehead of many toothed whales, dolphins, and porpoises.

pod A group made up of families of large, toothed whales.

resident pod A group of whales that stays in one area.

spyhopping Raising the head upright out of the water and sinking back into the water without a splash.

stranded Having come onto land alive or dead.

teats The parts of a mother's body through which the baby gets milk.

transient pod A group of killer whales always on the move.

63

Index

(**Boldface** indicates a photo, map, or illustration.)

Picture Acknowledgments: Front & Back Cover: © Tom Brakefield, Bruce Coleman Inc.; © Robert L. Dunne, Bruce Coleman Inc.; © Thomas Jefferson, Innerspace Visions; © Brandon Cole, www.norbertwu.com.

© Scott Benson, Marine Mammal Images 51; © Tom Brakefield, Bruce Coleman Inc. 5, 17, 41; © Brandon Cole, www.norbertwu.com 59; © Margot Conte, Animals Animals 57; © Will Darnell, Animals Animals 23; © Robert L. Dunne, Bruce Coleman Inc. 39; © Francisco Erize, Bruce Coleman Inc. 9; © Jeff Foott, Bruce Coleman Inc. 7; © John K. B. Ford, Ursus Photography 21, 35; © Werner Bertsch, Bruce Coleman Inc. 9; © François Gohier, Photo Researchers 31; © Robert W. Hernandez, Photo Researchers 21; © Thomas Jefferson, Innerspace Visions 61; © Johnny Johnson, Animals Animals 15; © Tom & Pat Leeson, Photo Researchers 19; © Eric Martin, Marine Mammal Images 33; © Amos Nachoum, Innerspace Visions 37; © Gregory Ochocki, Photo Researchers 53; © Brian Parker, Tom Stack & Associates 9; © Laura Riley, Bruce Coleman Inc. 9; © Betty Anne Schreiber, Animals Animals 4, 49; © Ingrid Visser, Innerspace Visions 29; © James D. Watt, Innerspace Visions 45; © F. Stuart Westmorland, Photo Researchers 13; © Glenn Williams, Ursus Photography 55; © Norbert Wu, www.norbertwu.com 43, 47.
Illustrations: WORLD BOOK illustration by Michael DiGiorgio 11, 25; WORLD BOOK illustration by Karen Donica 62.

Toothed Whale Classification

Scientists classify animals by placing them into groups. The animal kingdom is a group that contains all the world's animals. Phylum, class, order, and family are smaller groups. Each phylum contains many classes. A class contains orders, and a family contains individual species. Each species also has its own scientific name. Here is how the animals in this book fit in to this system.

Animals with backbones and their relatives (Phylum Chordata)

Mammals (Class Mammalia)

Whales (Order Cetacea)

Beaked whales (Family Ziphiidae)

Baird's beaked whale . . . . *Berardius bairdii*

Beluga and Narwhal (Family Monodontidae)

Beluga . . . . *Delphinapterus leucas*
Narwhal . . . . *Monodon monocerus*

Dolphins (Family Delphinidae)

Atlantic spinner dolphin . . . . *Stenella clymene*
Bottle-nosed dolphin . . . . *Tursiops truncatus*
Common dolphin . . . . *Delphinus delphis*
False killer whale . . . . *Pseudorca crassidens*
Killer whale . . . . *Orcinus orca*
Long-finned pilot whale . . . . *Globicephala melas*
Short-finned pilot whale . . . . *Globicephala macrorhynchus*
Spinner dolphin . . . . *Stenella longirostros*

Porpoises (Family Phocoenidae)

Dall's porpoise . . . . *Phocenoides dalli*
Finless porpoise . . . . *Neophocaena phocaenoides*
Vaquita . . . . *Phocoena sinus*

River dolphins (Family Platanistidae)

Amazon River dolphin . . . . *Inia geoffrensis*
Baiji . . . . *Lipotes vexillifer*